Financially
Fit

How to manage your money, get out of debt, build wealth, *and enjoy the Ride!*

A Three-Part Series

Book Two: 30 Days to Financial Fitness

By

Dr. Tony Pennells M.B.B.S, Dip. FS

By the Author

Dr. Tony Pennells M.B.B.S, Dip. FS

❧

Books

Financially Fit - Book One: How to Cure Money Stress

Financially Fit - Book Two: 30 Days to Financial Fitness

Financially Fit - Book Three: Your Path to Financial Freedom

Connect with me!

I love getting feedback from my readers and would really appreciate you taking a few minutes to post your comments or a brief review on my Amazon page.

https://www.amazon.com/author/drtonypennells

Also come join our Facebook community here:

Facebook - www.facebook.com/finfitwithdrtony

Thank you!

Disclaimer

General Advice Disclaimer

This book is presented solely for educational and general information regarding the subject matter covered. The author and publisher are not offering it as financial, legal, accounting, or other professional services advice. Whilst reasonable precautions have been taken to ensure the accuracy of the material contained herein at the time of publication, no person, persons or organisation should invest monies or take action on reliance of the material contained herein but instead should satisfy themselves independently of the appropriateness of such action.

No Warranties

While reasonable precautions have been used in preparing this book, the author and publisher make no representations or warranties of any kind and assume no liabilities of any kind with respect to the accuracy or completeness of the contents and specifically disclaim any implied warranties of merchantability or fitness of use for a particular purpose. Neither the author nor the publisher shall be held liable or responsible to any person or entity with respect to any loss or incidental or consequential damages caused, or alleged to have been caused, directly or indirectly, by the information or programs contained herein. No warranty may be created or extended by sales representatives or written sales materials. Every person is different and the advice and strategies contained herein may not be suitable for your situation. You should seek the services of a competent professional before beginning any improvement program. Some parts of the story and its characters and entities may be fictional. Any likeness to actual persons, either living or dead, is strictly coincidental.

Liability Disclaimer

The publishers, authors, and any other parties involved in the creation, production, provision of information, or delivery of this book specifically disclaim any responsibility, and shall not be liable for any damages, claims, injuries, losses, liabilities, costs or obligations including any direct, indirect, special, incide ntal, or consequential damages (collectively known as "Damages") whatsoever and howsoever caused, arising out of, or in connection with, the use or misuse of the book and the information contained within it, whether such Damages arise in contract, tort, negligence, equity, statute law, or by way of any other legal theory.

Published by: Doncarie Pty Ltd

Dedication

I dedicate this book to my two sons who inspire me to strive to become better.

Jarrod and Hudson, you are our future - may you stand on your mum and my shoulders as you reach for your dreams!

30 Days to Financial Fitness

Introduction

"In those days he was wiser than he is now; he used to frequently take my advice." ~ Winston Churchill

Where You Are

Welcome back to *Financially Fit*. I hope you enjoyed Book One, *How to Cure Money Stress*, but more than that I hope it left you a bit shocked at the generally poor financial condition of most people and nations.

When you realize how badly off the rest of the world really is, it can not only make you feel a little better about your own financial shortcomings and past mistakes, but can also help you realize how few people actually know and practice the rules that lead to good financial health.

This *Financially Fit* series is organized as follows:

- **Book One, How to Cure Money Stress** Understanding the past and getting you mentally aware and prepared before proceeding.

- **Book Two, 30 Days to Financial Fitness**: Handling money today; getting into a stable financial situation in the present and then gaining control. Even if you stopped after studying Book Two you would have a better understanding and more tools to be able to become financially fit than most people in the world today. Book Three however, offers much more. It gives you the tools you need for achieving true financial freedom.

- **Book Three, Your Path to Financial Freedom**: The philosophy and strategies for successful investing as well as creating new income streams and then protecting your wealth and passing it on. I also finish Book Three off with my perspective on practical answers to a number of frequently asked questions.

Let's take a moment to recap some of the key points covered in Book One.

Book One

One of the main outcomes of Book One was to reveal to you with stark contrast, the differences between those who know and understand the rules of financial fitness, from those who don't. The rules are really quite simple, but simple doesn't necessarily mean easy. They can be learned and applied by anyone, but does require the will to change old habits, and the discipline to follow through on your commitments to yourself. I've had students go from being deathly afraid to reveal their financial condition out of embarrassment, to deciding to be an advocate and help others after experiencing how quickly the can turn their finances around and dramatically improve their overall fitness through the same education you are receiving as a student of this series of books.

We covered the current state of affairs in the world around us and discussed the all-too recent global recession. We discussed some of the causes of these problems to help illustrate what to avoid in our personal lives.

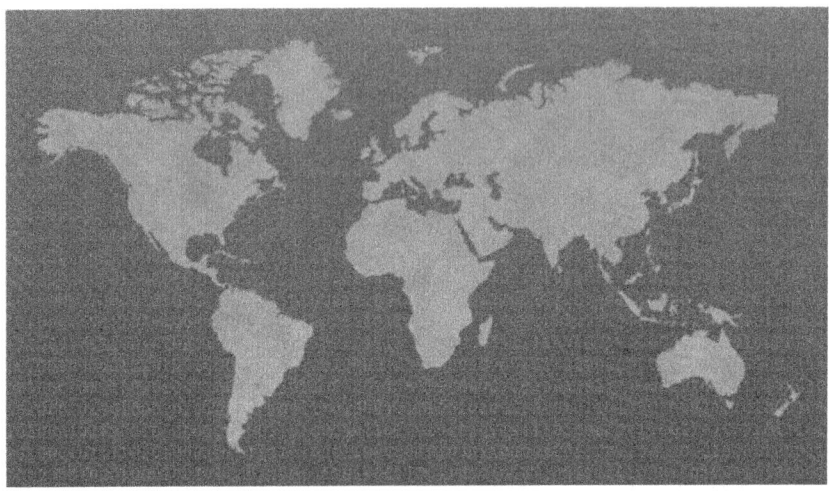

We examined and dismissed some of the most common financial myths. Looking over your existing paradigm – examining your current ideas on how money works - can be an extremely therapeutic exercise. It can result in new clarity and confidence when time-tested rules for good financial health replace those faulty beliefs.

We discussed some of the different values and habits of the different economic classes. The differences between the wealthy, middle-class, and the poor are far more than the size of their income and bank accounts. It begins with their personal philosophy, their values and habits – this is the foundation upon which financial independence and freedom is built. This alone can be eye opening, and I hope it was! Obviously we should only take advice from and copy those who have achieved what we want to achieve.

We have also aimed a large spotlight on the state of financial literacy in the world and in our own lives. The need for better, *practical* financial education is obvious.

I hope that it is now also extremely clear that we simply cannot rely on the government to provide any kind of quality of life for us in our retirement. If the entire world is so badly off, what would make us believe government retirement provisions and programs will even be available, much less sufficient, when we retire?

It all leads us to realize we must

- Rely on ourselves
- Get the education we need
- Take action today
- Make sure our plan is working and secure

- Help others do the same

So there's hope! *No matter where you are today, this minute, you can be financially fit in a month, and you can be financially FREE within a few years!*

Your past experience, education, successes and failures don't matter. I encourage you to leave them behind as we venture on into *real* and effective solutions for your finances that lead you to *financial fitness* – unencumbered by the stress and worry that hangs like a weight around so many people's necks.

Right Now

It starts with you.

Congratulations, once again, on your desire and commitment to learning how to become financially fit.

I believe that if we are personally financially healthy it simply makes for a better world. It is easier to focus on more fulfilling things in your life when your finances are not interfering with your every decision and hope.

In this book we will start by taking a look at your current situation. I suggest that you treat it as somewhat of an adventure that may reveal some of your personal habits and practices that have been holding you back.

We will then reveal the four pillars of wealth. These are the foundation principles that are *always* used by anyone who has ever become wealthy and maintained their wealth. We then spend some time working through how you can apply these principles into your own life. Coming out of this book you will have the necessary knowledge and understanding of exactly what you need to do to become *financially fit*. That is my promise to you.

I encourage you to take the time to consider the information that follows, and do the exercises as they come up.

Bon voyage!

Chapter 1

Now, About You…

"The thought manifests as the word,
The word manifests as the deed,
The deed develops into habit,
And habit hardens in character,
So watch the thought and its ways with care,
And let it spring from love,
Born out of concern for all beings…
As the shadow follows the body,
As we think, so we become"
~ Buddha (from the Dhammapada)

Introduction

From Book One you should be seeing how vital it is to take control of your financial future, and reach a resolute decision to change.

Wherever the word "change" is used, you should probably read "improve." It may be hard to "change" but easier to "improve." I like "improve" because anyone can usually see ways to improve. Ask someone to change, however, and this is often met with a mild panic attack!

The focus of our attention can turn now to your own past and current conditions while we cover some important things regarding yourself, relationships, children, and your own psyche.

You

A pretty philosophic question might be beneficial here. How defined are we by our past? Personally I can think of plenty I am proud of and plenty I would improve upon if given the opportunity.

We are known and judged by our past, there is no denying that. Regardless, we are alive today and we have a great deal of influence over our tomorrow. I like to think of my past as making me rich with experience, both good and bad. I believe that wisdom and strength comes from being honest with ourselves about our past, and in particular from reflecting on our thoughts, feelings and fears.

Normally we are our own harshest critics. We must be intelligent about which views we allow to occupy our daily thoughts and be conscious of whether they are helping us or harming us.

Relationships

Your past can come up and have a strong bearing on personal relationships as well. Open communication about finances during a relationship is a wise policy when you consider that many people cite financial stress and money problems as a main reason for relationship breakdown and divorce.

One of the first steps to open communication would be to put all the cards on the table and be honest about your financial past with your partner. Your credit and financial history can and will influence your relationship and even have a direct effect on a partner. Generally it is better to discuss these circumstances sooner rather than later. One way is to simply list all open debts, credit accounts and regular expenditures for each person. In this way there will less likelihood of any negative surprises on the horizon, and you are able to consider the whole financial picture when putting your *financial fitness plan* in place.

Some couples also find it useful to divide up the financial responsibilities according to each other's strengths, weaknesses, and interests. For example, a couple may benefit from small-scale specialization in checking a phone bill, seeing where they may get a better deal, or making smart selections at the grocery store.

I find that it is also important to openly share your financial goals and ambitions with your partner as early in a relationship as possible. To have honesty in this part of your relationship can be incredibly powerful, and can harness the combined strength of two people sharing the same journey. Equally if your partner has very different beliefs and values around money, then be very careful. In the latter circumstance, it could be a good idea to keep your money completely separate from your partner's money. You want to be sure that you are the master of your financial destiny at all times, especially if you are not certain that your partner is financially aligned with you.

Acknowledge your past and letting go

Be that as it may, your task now is to consider your financial past for a moment in all its glory and embarrassment, and acknowledge it.

Acknowledge that these things took place and also that you were responsible for them. If you can acknowledge responsibility, you then agree you had some degree of control over them. I believe in learning from our past. There are valuable lessons that you can bring with you if you take the time to consider them. It is important, however, that whilst you bring the lessons with you, you leave the negative emotions behind. You were being the best you that you knew how to be back then. Yes, I'm sure that you would like the opportunity to make different decisions if you had that time again, but that is where wisdom comes from.

Don't beat yourself up about decisions made in the past, but rather look at how you can invest those experiences into making better decisions today.

This is a critical step in our process of cleaning up your past, setting a new plan, and taking control of the present. We have our past, our present, and our future. Be transparent and honest with yourself about all three!

You have a second (or third or fourth) chance here with this series to start with the fundamentals that will make you financially fit and direct you firmly on the path to financial independence and freedom.

Commit

Now that we have looked behind us and acknowledged our past, a decision must now be made. A decision as to whether to stay the old course and keep doing things the way we have always done them, for more of same results, or to adjust our direction to head down a path that leads to financial freedom.

If no decision is made you will simply drift, as most people do in their financial lives, leaving their future to the mercy of decisions by others. So take the wheel, so to speak, and commit to becoming *financially fit.*

Commit to change and improve, and to do things differently to what has failed you in the past. Commit to working smart and hard for the benefits of becoming financially fit and experiencing the freedom you have in mind for you and your family. You will do this by taking one correct step at a time. You do not need to make all the changes overnight, but commit to become your own best friend, and remember – '*If it's to be, it's up to me!'*

Timeline

The decision to become *Financially Fit* can be reached in a split second. Developing the exact plan to follow can be created in no more than one to two weeks. Putting the plan into action should take no more than a month. Readjusting your habits to make them feel normal and automatic generally will take up to 90 days more.

As we progress you will realize how simple becoming financially fit actually is. The objective is eventually for you to be financially secure enough that having to work itself becomes an option.

Now let go of your past to free your hands for the future as we roll up our sleeves!

"We become what we think about all day long."
~ Ralph Waldo Emerson (US essayist & poet, 1803 - 1882)

Chapter 2

Personal Inventory

"A little more persistence, a little more effort, and what seemed hopeless failure may turn to glorious success." ~ Elbert Hubbard

It's now time to focus a bit more and see exactly where you are presently. Once you have this under your belt, you can continue with a real sense of where things currently are. This will also form a snapshot that you can revisit from time to time to see how far you have progressed from your starting point. There is a bit of work to be done here, however getting it done once will make it easier in the future.

It's time to take an inventory of

- Your mind
- Your money
- Your dreams

Your Mind

The following pages will take you through a series of thought-provoking questions designed to help open your eyes to unseen influences that may be impacting on your financial life.

I encourage you to try to look objectively on both the questions and your answers.

This evaluation of your past will show you what has worked and what hasn't. You should come out the other end enlightened with a new, deeper awareness of your own financial history and patterns. You will be able to identify specific influences, past advice, and habits that you may need to replace or modify in order to become financially fit.

The questions regarding your *mind* with regard to finance include the subjects of your

1. Education
2. Experience
3. Advice you have given and received

Write your answers on these or other pages, or at least relax and consider them without writing answers, and *enjoy!*

1. Education

a. How far did you go in school?

Did you enjoy it?

What of it do you use today?

What could you use today?

Would you like to go back?

b. What non-academic or other qualifications and training do you have?

Are you using them?

Would you like to?

c. What further education are you interested in?

Considering the cost and convenience, is it likely that you will undertake it?

d. Could you earn more income if you gained further education or skills?

2. Experience

A. Successes

What was your best or favorite job or business so far?

If you have ever owned your own business, what was that like?

Do you still own the business?

a. If yes, do you run the business, or does the business run you?

b. If no, did you make money when you sold the business?

Have you ever had any windfalls, or a sudden influx of lots of money?

a. How did you handle it?

b. What did you learn?

c. If you had it again, what would you do differently?

Do you have any investment experience?

a. What have you previously invested in?

b. How did that go?

c. Do you still have the investments?

d. Do the investments put money in your pocket, or cost you money?

B. Failures

Have you ever not known how you were going to buy food, or pay essential bills?

a. What were the circumstances in your life then?

b. How can you avoid finding yourself in that circumstance ever again?

Have you ever lost money on investments?

a. If yes, what happened?

b. What were you hoping to get out of the investments?

c. Why didn't this happen?

d. With hindsight, knowing what you know now, could you have avoided it?

Have you ever had to file for bankruptcy?

a. Why?

b. What happened as a result?

Have you ever had your house or car repossessed?

a. Why?

b. What happened as a result?

What do you wish you could do over and how?

3. Advice

a. Who has given you lots of advice in the past?

On reflection, was it good advice?

b. What advice has probably hurt you the most?

c. What advice would you give your children on finance?

d. If you could impart just one important piece of career advice to your children, what would it be?

e. Who do you currently take advice from?

f. Do they follow their own advice, and is it actually good advice?

Your Money

In this next section we will be taking a look at your current finances. This is an important step in taking control of your own personal money management and will go a long way in putting your entire life under more control.

Questions on finance include the areas of your

1. Income
2. Savings
3. Expenses
4. Debt

Again, you can write your answers or simply consider the questions. This section may take a little longer to complete, as I will be asking you to fill in amounts for your income and expenses (reasonable approximations are adequate for this exercise).

1. Income

a. What is your main source of income?

How much is your take-home pay every month?

b. What other sources of non-investment income do you have?

On average, how much do they bring in each month?

c. Do you have any investments?

Have you borrowed any money to buy the investments?

After borrowing costs, how much income do the investments bring in each month (if they cost you money, write your answer as a negative number)?

d. If you have a partner, what is their main source of income?

How much is their take-home pay each month?

e. Does your partner have other sources of non-investment income?

On average, how much do they bring in each month?

f. Does your partner have any investments?

Did they borrow any money to buy the investments?

After borrowing costs, how much income do the investments bring in each month (if they cost them money, write your answer as a negative number)?

g. What ways have you considered for raising your current income?

f. What other ways have you considered to earn more income?

*Note – even small increases in income can make a significant impact in both the certainty and the time to achieve financial security. The reason is that this increase used properly is *all surplus* income, and as long as you have the discipline to allocate it to *paying yourself first,* we can use this extra money to accelerate both debt reduction and wealth building.

2. Savings

a. Do you regularly save money?

If yes, how much do you save each month?

What are you saving for?

How much of your saving is investing to build wealth?

Do you save *every* month?

If not, why not?

Is your savings amount set up to be saved automatically?

b. Do you have a buffer or emergency account with at least 3 months of monthly expenses put aside?

c. What do you think the minimum amount is you should be saving every month?

How do you think at this point it might be easiest to do this (for example, online banking transfers, automatic deduction by your employer, and so on)?

Is there a way you can think of at this point to make saving automatic?

When you have achieved the *buffer* stage or financial security and happily have three months worth of bills saved in an emergency fund, you will be ready to start considering investments with the next goal of financial independence. What types of investments do you think you might look into in the near future?

3. Expenses

In this section we will be considering your expenses in the following general categories:

- Basic (or essential Expenses)
- Children (including education costs)

- Debt costs
- Flexible expenses

For a more accurate assessment, I invite you to download and complete the *Cash-Flow Manager* from my website.

a. Basic Expenses

How much do you spend on essential housing costs each month e.g. council rates, strata fees, electricity & water, essential maintenance, etc. (but <u>not</u> including your home mortgage payments)?

Essential transport costs each month e.g. petrol, parking, public transport costs, maintenance, registration (not including any finance costs)?

Essential groceries each month (not including luxuries or non-essentials and not including groceries for the kids)?

Essential health or medical costs each month?

Any other essential basic expenses?

b. Children

Do you have any children?

If so, how many and what ages?

If they are still dependent on you, at what age you do plan for them to be self-sufficient financially?

How much does their essential education cost each month (this is the bare essentials for their education)?

Do they go to private (non-government) school?

If yes, what does that cost on average each month?

How much do you spend on addition education expenses each month (e.g. tutoring)?

What do you spend on their sports and/or hobbies each month?

How much do you spend on their groceries each month (estimate as a proportion of your overall grocery costs)?

What are their average medical/dental costs each month?

What are their average monthly entertainment costs (e.g. movies, going out with friends etc.)?

How much do you spend on their clothing, etc. monthly?

How much would their travel and holidays cost per month (take annual amount and divide by 12)?

Any other expenses related to the children?

*Note – the reason that I ask you to consider the cost of the children as a separate component is two-fold:

- Firstly to help identify areas where you may be able to cut back to increase our allocation to paying yourself first, and
- Secondly to highlight that eventually they will (hopefully) be financially self-sufficient. When this time comes you get a financial windfall, as the money that you have previously been spending each month on the children is now available to accelerate our financial security strategy.

c. Debt Costs

Do you have a mortgage on your home?

How much do you currently owe?

What is the interest rate?

How much does it cost you each month?

Are you making more than the minimum monthly repayment to reduce this quicker?

If yes, how much extra are you currently paying over and above the minimum payment?

How long will it take you to own your home debt-free at your current repayment rate?

Do you have any car loans?

What do you currently owe?

What is the interest rate?

How much are the payments each month?

Are you making more than the minimum monthly repayment to reduce this quicker?

If yes, how much extra are you currently paying over and above the minimum payment?

How long will it take you to own your car/s outright at your current repayment rate?

Do you have any credit cards?

What is your limit on these cards?

If yes, do you pay them off in full each month?

If no, how much do you currently owe?

Are you still spending money on these cards despite not paying them off each month?

What are their interest rates?

How much are the payments each month?

Are you making more than the minimum monthly repayment to reduce this quicker?

If yes, how much extra are you currently paying over and above the minimum payment?

How long will it take you to pay off these cards at your current repayment rate?

Do you have any personal loans (include store loans for example 12 month interest free buy now, pay later offers)?

What do you currently owe?

What is the interest rate?

How much are the payments each month?

Are you making more than the minimum monthly repayment to reduce this quicker?

If yes, how much extra are you currently paying over and above the minimum payment?

How long will it take you to pay off these loans at your current repayment rate?

Do you have any student loans?

What do you currently owe?

What is the interest rate?

How much are the payments each month?

Are you making more than the minimum monthly repayment to reduce this quicker?

If yes, how much extra are you currently paying over and above the minimum payment?

How long will it take you to pay off these loans at your current repayment rate?

Do you have any investment debts?

How much do they cost you each month?

How much income do the investments bring in on average each month?

Overall do these investments put money in your pocket, or take money out of your pocket each month?

Do you have any other debts?

What do you currently owe?

What is the interest rate?

How much are the payments each month?

Are you making more than the minimum monthly repayment to reduce this quicker?

If yes, how much extra are you currently paying over and above the minimum payment?

How long will it take you to pay off these debts at your current repayment rate?

Now list all of the debts above and arrange them from smallest to biggest.

Now total up the amount that you are spending in debt repayments each month.

What proportion of your take-home pay goes in debt repayments each month (divide the total amount of debt repayment by your total monthly take-home income)?

Are you surprised by how much this is?

If you didn't have to make these payments each month, how much would you need to live on?

If you didn't have to make these payments each month, how much additional money would you have available to put towards becoming financially secure?

*Note – most people are truly shocked when they realize just how much of their take-home pay gets swallowed up by debt repayments. Getting out of debt is one of the first areas that we target. It is vital that you get this money back and available to put towards your financial security, not going into the banks pocket!

d. Flexible Expenses

These are things that you currently spend money on that, if you really had to, you could cut out (or at least cut down) and you would still survive. Consider the average monthly costs in the following areas:

Housing
Pay TV and gaming subscriptions?

Non-essential home decoration and renovation expenses?

Communication
Internet?

Mobile phone costs?

Transport
Car cleaning?

Non-essential car maintenance?

Shopping

Non-essential groceries and food luxuries?

Personal care costs

Personal care products?

Hairdressing?

Manicure/pedicure?

Massage/spa treatments?

Non-essential clothing / shoes, or other non-essential shopping items?

Newspaper and magazines?

Gifts / presents?

Pets?

Education

Non-essential personal or professional development?

Non-essential seminars and travel?

Health

Gym / sporting membership?

Non-essential health / medical costs?

Travel and Entertainment

Holidays?

Meals out?

Movies / Music?

Alcohol?

Cigarettes?

Other expenses

Donations / Charity?

Non-essential adviser fees?

Any other non-essential expenses?

*Note – if you are honest with yourself you can usually find numerous areas that can be cut out or cut back in the above areas. It is a balance of enjoying your life today, whilst still living within your means after paying yourselves first. It basically ends up coming down to how serious you are about your goal to become financially secure!

1. SUMMARY: Note that this is *not* a *budget*. This is just a snapshot so you know where you are starting from. With the information you have compiled above, calculate and fill in the following figures.

    a. Total of all monthly household income from all sources: $_____

    b. Total of all monthly expenses (total of basic, children, flexible and debt): $_____

    c. The difference – Hopefully positive, if negative put in (parenthesis): $_____

The difference between your income and expenses is called your *surplus.* Having a surplus is absolutely essential. It means that you are able to *live within your means,* a least theoretically (i.e. on paper). A rough estimation here of what your monthly surplus is will help you consider what you will be able to start diverting toward building financial security. This is a start. As you progress on the path of financial fitness, I will be showing you what you need to do to free up enough of a surplus to be sure you will become financially independent.

Your Dreams

In this final section of the chapter, we will spend some time crystallizing your dreams and setting some preliminary goals. This is what all the work is for in the first place! The goals you set here in this book will be further refined in Book Three.

"The quality, not the longevity, of one's life is what is important."

~ Martin Luther King, Jr.

1. Why are you studying *Financially Fit?*

2. What are you trying to achieve financially?

3. What are you trying to achieve where money or finances are holding you back?

4. What do you view as financial success?

5. If you didn't have to work for money what would you do?

   o   Where would you live?

6. If you were able to reduce work to 3 days per week without reducing your income, what would you do?

7. If you could afford to take 3 or more months off every year, what you would you like to do or accomplish?

8. What would give you financial peace of mind right now?

9. What would give you financial peace of mind in the future?

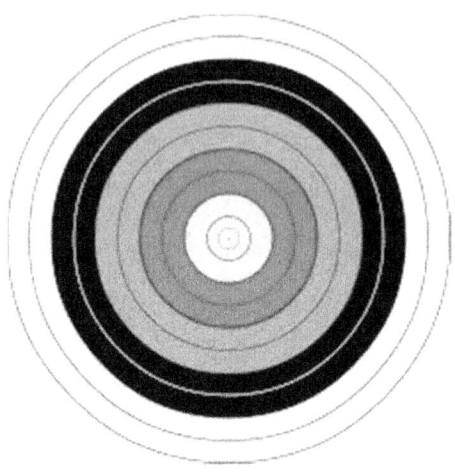

New Goals

At this time I would like you to take a moment to think about you answers above exactly what you would like to get out of this series. With this in mind, I would like you to write down one brief statement that describes what financial fitness would mean for you in six months' time, and then three specific, financial goals that fit with your statement on financial fitness. Include as many specifics as possible. Also include the dates or deadlines that you would like to accomplish them by.

Your statement should be written in the present tense and is even more effective if you can include an emotion. For example, a statement of financial fitness might sound like this:

*"After just six months I am really enjoying being financially fit
enough that I live my life with a great sense of financial well-
being. I no longer worry about money. All the bills are paid and
I love having a savings plan that is succeeding and on track for
my longer-term goals for investing and retirement. I am
confident I am finally on the right path and even feel capable of
advising others. Great change is no longer necessary. By
removing money as a daily concern, my life has risen to a new
level of quality and fulfillment."*

You will not be bound by what you write here, but the clearer
you are about the result you are looking to achieve, the easier it
is to create the specific plan that will get you there. Remember
that the clearer the mental picture is of the life you want to
create, the greater the likelihood is of you actually achieving
what you want!

Inspiration

NOTE: Much of this exercise is simply to get your mental machinery moving in certain directions. Inspiration, clarity and answers can often come when we least expect it. When you take the time focus and to work on something, you have more opportunity to be inspired and reach conclusions and bright ideas you might otherwise have not had.

So just have fun with this *inventory* for now. Do enter accurate detail where asked such as with your budget figures, but with others realize the purpose is simply to start you thinking about areas that might not have received your full attention before, and open the doors to inspiration over the next days and weeks.

Most of all, as with this entire series, take your time. Enjoy it as much as possible, for the more you do, the more valuable your results will be.

Chapter 3

The 4 Pillars of Wealth

"We are what we repeatedly do. Excellence, then, is not an act, but a habit." ~ *Aristotle*

Overview

It is important to remind yourself that people just like you have and currently are building strong financial walls around themselves and their families.

The basic rules around wealth are actually quite simple. Learning how to apply them in a clear, easy to follow personal plan is where the skill lies.

Taking control of how you manage your money today is the foundation upon which to build wealth, and in particular the type of wealth that progressively frees up your time.

The gift of giving you back the freedom over how you spend your time is my ultimate goal for you.

Right now, we will discuss the basic foundation of wealth building, however in *Book Three – Your Path to Financial Freedom–* I will be giving you the specific tools for investing and creating the passive incomes that allow you to become financially independent.

Good News

So let's kick things off with some good news: We all make enough money in our lives to be wealthy!

Think about that. I remember in high school, it was explained how many millions of dollars we would earn in the course of our careers, yet most people will neglect to become wealthy, possibly never realizing *millions of dollars* have slipped through their fingers!

Let's take a moment to reflect on the game of becoming financially independent. You become financially independent (and win the game) when you have built up passive incomes to the point where they are higher than your monthly living expenses. In other words, the game is to get yourself into a position as quickly as possible where your money is coming in without you working. At that point you will have your time freedom back.

The problem is that the vast majority of people have either never learned, or never understood the *Four Pillars of Wealth*: These are the foundation principles that the wealthy understand and apply – but here is the key insight to consider: They understood and applied these principles *before* they became wealthy. These are the foundations upon which they first started before becoming financially independent, and then they progressed to build larger wealth.

These are the four rules that need to be learned and mastered to be able to become *financially fit.*

The Four Pillars of Wealth

Let's now look at the *Four Pillars of Wealth – or the four fundamental rules of financial fitness.*

Rule 1 - Pay Yourself First

Rule 2 - Live Within Your Means

Rule 3 - Reinvest Your Investment Earnings

Rule 4 - Protect Yourself

These four principals are fundamental rules by which you should live your financial life. They are *how you get there.* In fact they are also *how you stay there.* These are the rules of the game called *money* or the game of *wealth.*

Given the right plan and enough time, just about anyone can achieve financial independence. The rules around becoming financially secure are actually quite simple. Most people complicate it either because they don't really know these simple rules themselves, or in particular, how to <u>specifically</u> apply these rules in their own circumstances.

We will spend the second half of this book looking at each of the Four Pillars of Wealth, and how they can be applied in your life.

Chapter 4

RULE #1: Pay Yourself First

"The individual has always had to struggle to keep from being overwhelmed by the tribe. If you try it, you will be lonely often, and sometimes frightened. But no price is too high to pay for the privilege of owning yourself." -- Friedrich Nietzsche

We all make enough money during our working life to be wealthy.

Many people feel that they are not paid enough while in reality the problem lies in the fact that they are not *keeping enough of what they earn.*

Did you know that over your life you will probably earn *well over four million dollars*? This is true if we assume that the average household income is $100,000 per year, and you work from the age of twenty-one until the age of sixty-five.

So why do so many people struggle with money during their working life? Why do even more people have barely enough money to exist in their retirement, often only getting by with the support of a government program or small pension?

It doesn't have to be that way if you remember that the game is making sure that when you are no longer able to, or want to work, you have enough money invested and earning enough passive income to provide for you.

To accomplish this from now on a part of every dollar you earn *must* be saved for your future.

This brings us to *Rule 1: Pay Yourself First.*

The wealthy follow this rule and make sure that they always pay themselves first.

They keep a portion of every dollar they earn for themselves - that is, for their *future* selves. They do not spend that money for any reason *today*. This money is <u>not</u> being saved to buy a car, holiday, upgrade or renovate their home, nor save for a holiday. Its sole purpose is to be invested - to be sent out to work, to go earn more money and grow in value so that their future is financially secure.

Yes, before anyone else - including even their rent or mortgage payment, school bills, and even the groceries - they pay themselves first!

The River

Imagine the money you earn each month as a river. Now also imagine that the water in the river is the *only* source you have to provide you with everything you need not only for today, but also for the future.

Most people just take from the river as they go, buying food, clothes, travel, etc. without a clear understanding of what the purpose/s of the river actually is. They also don't think about how much they can take from the river before there is no more water left to use (until the next rainfall or pay day).

Along the course of the river, there are also a lot of people and companies that want to take some of your money away, and unless you are paying yourself first, before they can get their hands on it, they usually succeed!

Unless you have the habit of *paying themselves first*, in other words making sure that the first water that you take from the river is saved for a rainy day (or in this example, a time when there is no rain!), there usually is no water left in the river after everyone else has been to the river for their "needs".

Your income is not just for living today; it is for living today and providing for tomorrow.

How many people all over the world violate this principle their entire life? Not only do they use all of their own *river water* but even borrow great amounts from others, usually to buy things that they don't truly *need*!

That's actually kind of stupid when you look at it that way, right?

Who in their right mind would ever waste all of the water they have just because they are a bit thirsty now, and hope that if they ever get thirsty again (an absolute certainty) that others will always be happy to give them some of their own precious water?

Your river should have off-shoots, or channels at the very beginning of the river that flow out to a dam of investments that make their own money. When the dam is full enough and big enough, you get to a point of not needing the river anymore.

In literal terms, *working* becomes a choice. You would not need to work anymore, as your dam is now big enough to look after not only your current needs, but your future ones as well.

Imagine that!

The wealthy intimately know and practice this key first principle. They know that while they are working they have a river of money flowing - they know that right now they have their cash-flow. They also know that some of that river must flow into a dam of investments that then makes its own money.

When their dam is big enough, it makes them enough money for them to have the choice of working or not working as they see fit.

The big mistake that most people make – and over ninety out of every one hundred people don't ever become financially secure - is that they either ignore or don't know that they need to be paying themselves first. Even if they do, they may not know how much they should be putting away.

As a result, they end up breaking Rule 2. They *live beyond their means*, spending all of the money they earn today - and sometimes even more than they earn, borrowing from their credit cards or from loans and keeping nothing for themselves.

This leaves them either not enough or nothing at all flowing into the dam.

Your challenge is to make sure that enough money is flowing into your dam. Succeed and your chances of becoming financially free skyrocket. Fail and you will almost certainly never become financially independent.

The first step is to make sure that you are *regularly* paying yourself first. The next part is to make sure that the amount you are paying yourself is enough to ensure that you achieve your future goals. This requires a little calculation. Of course if you're reading this series and you're twenty-years old, you will have a different calculation than if you are now fifty years old or older. *Both* plans can succeed, but the amounts needed to save are different.

Income

This brings up the usual objection,

"I'm not making enough income to save or invest!"

The exact opposite is true. The real problem, rather than the amount of income a person makes, is that they are not keeping enough (or any) of the money they do earn. This is almost always due to the fact that they are trying to pay themselves <u>*last*</u>. As we've already discussed, no matter what you earn, most people find things to spend their money on, and spend up to (or a little over) what they earn. In many cases they convince themselves that these are actually things they *need,* rather than the "wants", or luxuries that they truly are. Think about this – no matter what people earn they almost never have any money left over at the end of the month to save.

It's not what you make; it's what you keep!

Compare for a moment two people, one earning $200,000 a year and another earning just $40,000 a year. Many doctors and lawyers by their own admission:

"... make $200,000 a year and spend $250,000 a year."

If the person earning $40,000 a year saves just 10% he would have *something* ($4,000 at the end of the first year) but the *rich-guy* would have only *debt*!

In fact if you make relatively little, it is actually easier to get to a position of financial security. This is because your monthly expenses are lower, and therefore your investments don't need to be earning that much before they can cover those expenses and set you free.

The hard part is making the decision that "if it's to be it's up to me". Stop making excuses, decide not to be a victim and put the disciple in place to pay yourself first. We can then show you how to apply intelligence to what funds you do have and get them working hard to provide for your future. The good news is that you can indeed do this, as many have done before and are doing now, despite tight circumstances.

The trick is to make it a habit to save, then a habit and a skill to invest. But I'm going to show you how to make it even easier than that. We discussed *consciously* forming habits in Book One. We're going to take it a step further and make your saving *automatic.* In fact unless you *pay yourself first automatically*, as the wealthy do, you are most likely going to struggle unnecessarily with making the principle of *Paying Yourself First* a success habit.

So how much should I be paying myself?

It's very important to be sure that the amount you are putting away is enough to reach your goal of becoming financially independent. But, at the same time, if you start off too ambitiously, your plan may fail. The key is to find the right balance between being able to enjoy your life today <u>and</u> put away enough for your future needs.

It is okay to start conservatively if you then monitor your cash flow and regularly look for opportunities to increase what I will call your *savings standard*, or how much you should currently be paying yourself.

It is perfectly okay to pay yourself, by the way. Very few people work without pay!

There are a number of factors that need to be considered when figuring out just how much to pay yourself, such as:

- How much you currently have invested.
- How much debt you currently have.
- How many more years you plan to be working.
- What income you want when you are no longer working.
- What type and mix of investments you feel comfortable with – this will affect the rate of return you are likely to be able to get from your investment portfolio.
- How much you eventually want to leave your kids or estate.

I recommended that you take the time to find and work with a trustworthy advisor (not always easy to find unfortunately) to help you calculate and confirm the minimum amount you need to be paying yourself. Also, visit my website for some free tools that can help you.

As a rule of thumb numerous financial experts have suggested that if you can save on average 15% of your before-tax income into a balanced mix of investments over your entire working life that you could reasonably look to retire on an income of around two-thirds of your salary, and expect this income to last around 30 years or so.

It is important to note that they use a figure of 15% of your *before tax income* above. This is the amount you are earning before you pay any personal income tax. This is a different number if you look at the amount you should be saving from your take-home pay.

For example – let's use a person earning $50,000 per year in before tax income, and assume that they pay around 20% in personal income tax.

- $50,000 before tax income
- $10,000 income tax paid
- $40,000 after-tax income or take-home pay
- $7,500 is the savings amount that 15% represents

- 18.75% is the amount of take-home pay that should be saved to equal the same as 15% of before-tax income saved.

As a general rule, I like to use a minimum of **20%** of people's take-home pay as the target for clients to be paying themselves first. I find that we can usually achieve some amazing goals over time when they are saving at or above 20% of their take-home pay.

Now – please don't get discouraged when you see that figure. First of all it may not be realistic for you to get to that point in one step and keep balance in paying all your bills today. Also remember that we are all at various stages of life – at times we have less demands or real needs on our income, and at other stages, such as when our kids are dependent on us, we have more demands. What you can see is that it is a meaty goal that will need to be taken seriously to have a real chance of begin accomplished.

"A journey of a thousand miles begins with a single step" –
Chinese philosopher, Lao-tzu

The key to successfully achieving any substantial goal is to start. Begin with where you are, with whatever you can. We will look to accelerate and increase your *savings standard* step-by-step until it is at the right number for you.

The other key point is that you may not be on your own in reaching your savings standard. The minimum amount that you are actually responsible for paying yourself can depend on whether you are an employee or working for yourself.

I'm an Employee

The great news is that if you are employed and working for someone else there is a good chance that your employer is already making payments into a retirement account for you.

In Australia it is currently mandatory for employers to pay a minimum of 9.25% of workers' wages into a superannuation fund or retirement account. This mandatory amount is gradually being increased to 12% over the next few years. This is great news, especially for the younger workers in Australia, as it represents a big chunk of the amount you are paying yourself already.

The amount employers' pay into retirement accounts on your behalf varies greatly depending on which country you live in. You should verify how much, if any, that your employer is paying into a retirement account on your behalf. As a rule of thumb then, you should take responsibility for saving the remainder up to the 20% of your take-home pay (or the amount that represents your actual number).

To be clear, you can consider any payments that employers pay into your retirement accounts to be part of the *pay yourself first* amount. You then need to make up the difference. For example, if your employer is paying an amount equal to 10% of your take –home pay, then you should be saving the additional 10% yourself.

If at first you need to start with a smaller amount to make paying yourself sustainable, *that is okay as well*. The important thing is to *start,* and to start creating good habits as well as creating investment funds.

I'm Self-Employed

If you work for yourself then chances are that you do not have an employer making any superannuation or other retirement fund payments for you. This means that you need to be paying yourself the *twenty percent* or more of your take home pay.

Again, <u>*if at first you need to start with a smaller amount to make 'paying yourself' sustainable, that is okay as well*</u>, however I suggest that you try to start off with paying yourself at least 10% of your take-home pay. The important thing is to *start* creating good habits as well as creating investment funds.

How do I actually pay myself first?

It is critically important that you actually do pay yourself, and that you pay yourself first before paying any other bills or expenses (including rent and mortgage payments!) otherwise there is great risk you will not be paid (by you) at all. I cannot over-emphasize how important this is. Without a conscious decision to do this almost everyone will have a tendency to pay themselves last - it's unfortunately the nature of how we tend to handle finances.

Once you have worked out the exact amount you will be paying yourself first, then next step is to setup these payments run *automatically*. The simplest way to do this is to set up these payments via internet banking.

If you don't have internet banking, you should visit your local banker to see if it might be set up for you, or perhaps even seek an alternative bank where this is possible. You may also be able to ask your employer to make the payment for you from each pay packet.

Where should these payments go?

I suggest that you set up a separate bank account especially for your pay yourself first payments. It should be used for no other purpose, and should not be mixed with any other money. I recommend that you look for an account that has low or no ongoing bank fees and pays regular interest. It is also very important that it is not easy for you to draw money out from this account – in other words it should have no bank (ATM) card, credit card, cheque book etc. attached to the account. You want money going into this account, and not ever coming out, except to build investments that will make you passive income.

You can call this account something that will always remind you of its purpose, for example – Surplus Account, Wealth Account, Future Fund, or *PYF (pay yourself first) Account.* I'll be calling it your *PYF account* from this point on. I will be going into more detail around how we structure and further use this *PYF Account* in Book Three.

When should I be making these payments?

Set up your savings amount to go automatically into your *PYF Account* no later than three days after your pay is scheduled to arrive (for example, if you are normally paid on the first of the month, then set up to pay yourself automatically on the third of the month). This will allow for small variations on the day your pay actually arrives in your bank account, around weekends, or other delays like bank holidays and so on.

Be sure to transfer your 'Pay Yourself First' amount to your PFY Account before you pay any other bills!

At the risk of being repetitious, I strongly recommend that you pay yourself first *automatically,* so that it happens each and every month without you having to remember or think about it. That by definition is a *good habit.*

Unless you set a plan to pay yourself first *automatically*, you may be setting yourself up to fail unless you are one of those rare and disciplined people who can be sure that they will pay themselves *first*, each and every month.

I can share with you that in the beginning when I made the commitment to pay myself first I worked out the exact amount I needed, but didn't set it up so that it happened automatically. I thought that I was disciplined enough to do it myself. I wasn't! Over the first 12 month I only actually paid myself first in 3 of the 12 months. The other 9 months I had some excuse, usually some 'unexpected' bill that I allowed to take priority over my financial future. What I eventually realized was that I was still paying myself <u>last</u>. The process only began to work properly when I set-up the "pay yourself first" payment to be paid automatically on the third day after my income usually arrived. This worked. Before I could think about it I had paid myself first automatically and regularly. Within 90 days I had adjusted the rest of my lifestyle to live on what remained in my normal bank account after I had paid myself first. In fact after 90 days I hardly noticed any difference in my lifestyle at all!

If you make the commitment to pay yourself first, you will quickly find that you *can* enjoy your life today, in many cases without noticeably curbing the lifestyle you currently enjoy, and be on a plan that builds your future financial security.

It's well worth repeating that you will soon enough notice:

- the amount of money in your *PYF Account* quickly builds, making you less vulnerable to any financial emergencies,
- you are a little wealthier every month,
- that over time your money is starting to work *for you* and starting to earn some decent money itself!
- Most importantly, your *financial peace of mind* begins to noticeably develop.

The peace of mind that you will experience and the confidence from being in control of this important part of life goes a very long way to improving the quality of life today, while ensuring a better life for you tomorrow as well.

You deserve to be paid for the work that you do. You deserve to keep a part of what you earn. And if these reasons are not good enough, you will be sorry if you don't!

Remember, the money you make today is for today *and* for tomorrow. Even the beasts of the wild, dogs, and squirrels know this as they hide food for a rainy day, to give them a more certain source of food in the future.

Ultimately the most exciting part of *paying yourself first*, is that *this* is the source of your investments. Without this step in place, we cannot go into the types of investments that regularly put passive income into your pocket. Remember that this is actually what the game of money is about – having investments that earn enough passive income to give you the choice not to work.

A must-have classic book that should be on your shelf and read at regular intervals is *The Richest Man in Babylon by George S. Clason*; its engaging stories effectively drive this principal home.

Children

I'd like to finish this chapter off with my thoughts on teaching your children to understand the value of money and the rules to financial success.

As soon as your child is able to earn their own money, even if it is working around the home for their allowance, I suggest that you have them apply the rules of '*part of all they earn is theirs to keep (for their future),* and '*pay themselves* first'.

A good starting plan is to put aside no less than 30% of every dollar into a savings account. You will be amazed how quickly this can start to grow if you don't touch the savings. A great plan is to show your child the interest that the money is earning each and every month, and how the interest grows as you send the money out to work each month.

My wife and I have done this with our kids. From a fairly young age they have had clear understanding that if they keep sending their money out to work it will earn money (e.g. interest earned if it is in a savings account). If you don't spend the interest, but instead also send the interest out to work, you will have more money working for you, earning even more interest. If you keep doing this, eventually you will have enough money going out to work each month that you will not need to work.

If you can start this with your kids as early as possible, not only will you be teaching them good money habits (and it is far easier to do this right from the start, rather than trying to change bad habits once they have already been learned!), but you will also be giving them many years head start in their journey to become financially free. This will greatly increase the chance of them not only becoming wealthy, but passing these new habits down for generations to come. What a gift!

Chapter 5

RULE #2: Live Within Your Means

"Annual income twenty pounds, annual expenditure nineteen six, result happiness. Annual income twenty pounds, annual expenditure twenty pounds ought and six, result misery." - Charles Dickens, David Copperfield

Living within your means is not as bad as it sounds!

I am always happily amused at how many people who finally sit down and compile a home cash-flow management plan (notice we did not say *budget*) are shocked at how much money is being wasted. When they realize this, it is then a fairly simple step for them to choose to take control over where their money is being allocated.

Even if the surplus in the plan is tight, they are now able to divert that *flow of river* that was going every month to two expensive coffees per day, for example, to just one expensive coffee every other day and increase the amount they can allocate to '*paying themselves first*'.

And even when people are confronted with a completely upside-down situation where they are bringing in much less than they need, it is almost always the case that they knew or suspected this was the case anyway!

The difference is that now they know how bad the situation actually is and can actually do something about it. Neglecting such a situation can literally end up in bad health, divorce court, or much worse.

This is the same as looking in the mirror without our clothes on for an accurate view of ourselves. If we have been living life with a few too many excesses, it is important to have an honest reflection. We probably need to cut back and increase our exercise a bit if we are serious about wanting to live a long, healthy life.

Where did it All Go?

In Book One and earlier in this book, we examined where our money goes in pretty good detail. In fact we looked and discussed the change in spending patterns over a fifty-year period. In general our money is going to support four main areas:

- Basic living expenses
- Expenses associated with raising the children
- Debts (*Housing debt, consumer debt* and Investment Debts)
- Flexible or lifestyle expenses

Consumer debt includes the monthly heavy interest and principle (often upwards of 22%) *wasted* on goods and services that are often classifiable as *wants* rather than *needs*.

There is nothing wrong with wanting to enjoy life, but there is something wrong with waste and with consumption out of proportion to one's income.

Most people spend first and save or invest last. No matter how hard they budget there is usually nothing left to regularly invest.

As humans we have been given the gift and curse of imagination and desires. We will always have goals, dreams, and ambitions that add up to more than we can afford. Think about this carefully. Almost every day we hear about celebrities and "rich people" declaring bankruptcy or experiencing some other financial difficulty – despite earning millions of dollars a year. How can someone get into financial trouble on that type of income ... *"I mean seriously!!!"?*

In almost all cases their desires, goals and ambitions have outgrown their income. They have come to believe that what they truly *'need'* is a multi-million dollar home, or homes in several countries, butlers and servants, private planes, and perhaps even their own major league sports team. These needs took priority over making sure that they were first financially secure, and secondly *living within their means.*

Now I'm not for one minute suggesting that we should sacrifice our enjoyment of life today, in fact far from it. The key is to prioritize which of our goals, dreams and ambitions are the most important to us, AND can fit into our current means (after we have *paid ourselves first*). We can then set goals and targets to increase what we currently earn, so that we can go after other goals AND accelerate our journey to financial security *at the same time*.

Don't Budget

Budgets just don't work!

What does work is *paying yourself first, and then living on what's left.* Quite seriously, I can say without reservation that as a professional advisor in the field of finance, budgets almost never work.

If you try to budget, then what you are trying to do is control your spending so that you have a little left over at the end of the month.

This is fundamentally wrong for two reasons:

1. Budgets generally don't tell you what you should do with the money you are supposed to have left at the end of the month, and
2. Budgets are teaching you that you should pay yourself *last*, after you have paid everyone else.

Generally, budgets almost never achieve their promised outcome of helping you to have extra money at the end of each and every month. What they are very good for, however, is making you feel incredibly guilty that you can't stick to something as simple as a budget!

Again, the first two rules to becoming financially secure are:

1. Pay yourself first
2. Live within your means

That is, learn to live on what is left *after you have paid yourself first. This cannot be stressed often enough in this series.*

If you follow these two rules, it almost doesn't matter what you spend your money on, so long as you don't spend more than you have left *after* paying yourself first.

If you follow just these two rules, over time you will become wealthier.

Needs vs. Wants

Let's really start understanding needs versus wants - what is truly a *need* and what is really just a *want*?

You will always have desires greater than your ability to earn. This is human nature. Any person or group will always try to spend more than it makes.

This might not now seem realistic, but many of us could happily live on less than we are spending at the moment. Think about it. Most of us have been working for more than a couple of years and chances are that you are earning more today than what you were earning just three to five years ago, yet it still feels like we never quite have enough money.

I was recently speaking with a very dear friend of mine (let's call her Kate).

Kate is a single mum working very hard and doing a great job on raising her teenage daughters, however she is doing it tough financially.

We got onto the subject of money, and the principles of becoming financially secure. We worked out that she needed to be paying herself a minimum of $1200 per month to have a realistic chance of being financially independent by her desired retirement age.

She told me she just didn't earn enough money for her to realistically save any money at the moment, let alone $1200 per month, saying, "Maybe when my daughters are off my hands I can start saving properly". I argued back saying that the problem was not how much money she was making, but rather that she wasn't *keeping enough of what she earned.*

It basically came down to the fact that she didn't believe that it was possible to pay herself first.

I asked her if she was prepared to show me where her money was currently going. Kate agreed, and we sat down and filled in the first part of my cash flow management system – a spreadsheet that itemized how much is being spent on various areas.

What it showed was that she had a very small surplus of around $150 each month – this was not allowing for unexpected expenses. When Kate saw this, she looked at me and said, "I told you I didn't have any money to save". I asked Kate if she could look me in the eye and tell me that every single dollar was being spent on things that truly *needed*. She said, of course not, but what luxuries she did spend money on didn't amount to much.

She agreed to work with me on the second part of the cash-flow management system, which looks for areas that we can cut back, cut-out, or restructure.

It took about two hours, but what we found were agreed areas that could be realistically cut back without much hardship. These cutbacks freed up just over $1000 per month. In addition she had 2 personal loans and a maxed out credit card that was costing her $904 per month in minimum payments.

I suggested to Kate that if she applied 2/3 of the new surplus to accelerating the repayment of these loans she would be debt free in 8 months, and could then save the entire $2000 per month to her *PYF account.*

If Kate follows this advice she could be looking at having around $1,500,000 available in retirement!

Achieving wealth is usually not because we don't have enough money. In fact, there are probably many people in your suburb that get by just fine earning quite a lot less than you. The basic problem is that we are not following the correct plan.

Often we confuse what we need to sustain basic living with wants.

A want is anything above the basics of what we need to get by.

For example:

- A nicer home than we need
- Buying new furniture, as well as any decorative items for the house
- Driving a nicer car than we need
- Private schooling
- Pay television
- Regular dining out, in fact possibly *all* dining out
- Holiday spending
- Internet gaming subscriptions
- Most memberships
- Magazine subscriptions

- And much more!

Time spent honestly looking over what things you spend money on today could mean a better life for you and your family tomorrow. Start including in your calculations how it will feel to be able to pay for a child's education without worry, to take the family on a vacation without worry, and to have the freedom of time to travel the world with your partner rather than travel around your own city.

That said, I am actually not suggesting that we need to stop spending on all of the wants and luxuries that we enjoy. What I am saying is that being financially fit means being able to enjoy the desires that can fit into the budget that you've set in order to live within your means.

In other words *pay yourself first* and then spend what's left.

You can use your new cash-flow management system to:

- Work out what are the essentials or needs that you do need

- Discover what the more preferred wants are that you can actually fit into the amount of cash you have left over *after* you have allowed for your needs.

The key is to live within your means: only go on holidays that are within your means, only buy a car that is within your budget. If there are more wants that you feel are important to you, then you need to figure out how you can earn more, or free up more cash, to give you the ability to have them, but only after you have *paid yourself first*.

This can be easier than you think.

Reality Check

So if you really had to, what is the minimum income you could live on?

Warning: If you don't develop the habit of paying yourself first and then living within your means, you may very well get the chance to find out how little you could live on – when you don't have retirement savings and have to depend on family and friends, or a lousy government pension! This is not what I want for you.

At the time of writing this, in Australia the old age pension is currently:

Status	Pension Rate per fortnight	Pension rate per year
Single	$689.00	$17,914
Couple	$519.40 each	$27,009 (combined)

(Source: www.centrelink.gov.au, 14 November 2011. Note: the above amounts exclude the pension supplement, which is a maximum of $59.80 a fortnight for singles and $90.20 a fortnight for couples.)

Upon seeing the above figures you should be saying to yourself, "That doesn't apply to me! I have no intention of just living on the pension!"

So let's look then at another source of interesting if alarming information, The ASFA Retirement Standard.

This is research done by the Association of Superannuation Funds of Australia, which regularly looks at the weekly and annual budget needed by Australians to fund either a comfortable or modest standard of living in the post-work years. It provides detailed breakdowns of what single people and couples need to support their chosen lifestyles.

We happen to think that this can also be very useful as a guide to compare what you are currently spending and help to see where *wants* have crept in. In particular it's helpful if you cannot see where you can cut back enough to be able to *pay yourself first.*

	Modest lifestyle - single	Modest lifestyle - couple	Comfortable lifestyle - single	Comfortable lifestyle - couple
Housing - ongoing only	$55.96	$53.71	$64.85	$75.18
Energy	$30.62	$40.67	$31.08	$42.15
Food	$72.78	$150.75	$103.97	$187.14
Clothing	$17.62	$28.61	$38.14	$57.22

Household goods and services	$26.02	$35.28	$73.19	$85.74
Health	$33.12	$63.92	$65.71	$115.97
Transport	$88.63	$91.14	$132.07	$134.59
Leisure	$73.03	$108.80	$221.31	$303.28
Communications	$9.16	$16.03	$25.17	$32.04
Total per week	$406.94	$588.91	$755.49	$1,033.31
Total per year	$21,218	$30,708	$39,393	$53,879

(Source: ASFA Retirement Standard June 2011)

The above table assumes that you own your own home without a mortgage. You will also need to allow for children - if you have dependent children - and education if relevant.

Remember the goal of the game:

When you no longer can, or no longer want to work, to have enough money invested and earning money for you, so you have that choice!

- Rule 1: Pay yourself first
- Rule 2: Live within your means

As long as you are paying yourself enough and applying Rule 3, which is sending your money out to work for you (and reinvesting what it earns – Rule 3), you can happily spend the money that is left on whatever *wants* or luxuries you desire.

The above table can be a bit of a reality check on what is truly a need versus a *want*. It could reasonably be said that everything spent over and above *modest lifestyle* amounts are *discretionary* or *wants*. These *wants* don't necessarily need to be cut out or cut back, unless you cannot put the required amounts aside to *pay yourself first.*

Did You Know?

The most common reason people come out of retirement is financial need - they run out of money! (Source: ABS)

Did You Know?

65% of Australians have spent all of their superannuation or retirement savings by age seventy-five. (Source: Australian Investment Institute, 2011)

If you cannot live on this type of budget now, how will you survive on it in the future, when you are no longer working? Make the decision to pay the price now - It's *less* painful! In fact it is usually not only very livable, but gives you better peace of mind and a better quality of life.

- Work out how much you need to be *Paying Yourself First*.
- Commit to *Living within Your Means*, by getting your cash-flow management in order.

"*That sounds like a tall order! How do I actually do it?*"

Cash-Flow Management vs. Budgeting

Rule Two, Living Within Your Means, can be alternatively stated as *managing your cash-flow*.

What a cash-flow management system does is a little different to a budget.

Begin with your *Pay Yourself First* goal

The first step in a cash-flow management system is to work out the goal, or objective that you are trying to achieve – in other words – what is the goal *Pay Yourself First* amount you are aiming for.

Once you have set the goal for the amount you should be paying yourself, a cash-flow management system can do the following:

- Help you see or find out where your money is currently going.
- Help you see what your essential expenses are. *Essential expenses* are the necessities in life like putting a roof over your head, buying essential clothes, and having food on the table.

- Help you to set limits on how much you can spend on wants and luxuries. Remember, you will have already paid yourself first, so this helps in two ways:
  - o Makes sure you don't go into any more debt, such as overspending on credit cards, and
  - o Helps see where you may comfortably cut back, so you can allocate a little more to paying yourself.

- Help you see other areas that could be improved, such as:
    - Put in place a debt-termination program to accelerate paying off debt
    - Your mortgage: Review how much interest you are paying to the bank and consider what a difference refinancing your loan could make.

A.B.C.D.E.F. of Cash-Flow Management

Cash-flow management can be summarized and understood by the letters A.B.C.D.E.F.

Consider the following formula:

$$E - A = B + C + D + F$$

Let me expand:

Earned income minus *Abundant or surplus cash* = *Basic expenses* plus *Children's expenses* plus *Debt costs* plus *Flexible expenses*

Earned income is the money that you earn from your work or personal exertion.

Abundant or *surplus cash* is the money that you can put aside for your future needs (the money you use to *pay yourself first*).

Basic expenses are what it costs for your basic needs, such as basic [not luxury] food, shelter and clothing. This does not include spending sprees on new shoes, brand names, or sales. That type of spending should be included in flexible expenses. I also do not count the costs of housing loans in this category, as this is a debt cost, and one that I want you to eliminate as soon as you reasonably can.

Children's expenses are the costs or expenses that you have when raising your children. I like to consider it as a separate category for a couple of reasons. Firstly, your basic expenses increase when your children are financially dependent on you, as do your flexible expenses. Secondly, you have a new expense category in education costs. Most importantly though, by keeping this as a separate category it allows you track the decrease to your cost of living when your children are out of school and no longer a financial drain on your income.

Debt costs are the monthly costs that pay for your loans. It is vitally important that you separate these expenses out, so that you can see exactly how much of your take-home pay is being absorbed by these costs. This is often where you can find big chunks of cash being wasted every month in interest costs for consumer debts and large home mortgages!

Flexible expenses are what you spend on the 'wants' of your life. These are not basic needs – even if you argue that you cannot live without them, the reality is that they are still flexible. If you really had to, you could cut out or reduce some, or all of these expenses, and life would still go on.

The *second step* in cash-flow management system is to list where they are currently spending their money, and allocate these expenses into the categories above (i.e. are they a basic cxpense, children's expense, debt cost, fixed expense, etc.).

The third step is to look closely at each expense and identify areas that you could reduce or cut-out all together.

It is very common when people start applying the *Financially Fit Cash-Flow Management System* that they begin to see better ways of allocating the money they already have, not to mention come up with new ways to earn more income.

They will often find cash by looking at how much money they are giving to the banks through mortgage payments, other loan payments, and credit card interest every month. By aggressively reducing debt, which will be covered later, you can often free up *thousands* of dollars that can then be applied to achieving financial freedom and improving your peace of mind.

While it may take a few years to actually terminate your mortgage; a refinance and a debt termination plan involving your other debts can free up a large amount of cash-flow in a matter of just weeks or months.

The *fourth step* is then to total up the potential savings you have identified in step three, and see if it enough for you to reach your *Pay Yourself First* amount. Most people are pleasantly surprised to see that there is more than enough identified savings to be able to confidently set-up a regular *automatic* Pay Yourself First amount. If after an honest, hard look you can see that you cannot reach your savings goal, then see where you can start – and start there. Then finally set-up a task or action items list on what you need to cancel or cut-out, and what your weekly spending limit is on the various items.

Remember my view is that budgets don't work. What does work is to *pay yourself first*. The main aim of the cash-flow management system is to help you see that you do have the ability to pay yourself first. Most people are surprised to discover that they definitely could be paying themselves first, but are surprised to see how much money just seems to evaporate out of their wallets on a myriad of small expenses such as pricy lunches, gourmet coffees, and so on. Just setting some weekly limits in these areas can bring back as much as a few hundred dollars each and every month. By prioritizing what you spend your money on, most people do not even notice the difference in their lifestyle within 90 days. In fact you may even have more fun taking more care and pride on choosing what deserves your hard earned cash.

If you feel you need any extra help, the *Financially Fit Cash-Flow Management System* is the perfect first step to assist you with *Paying Yourself First* and *Living within Your Means.* Visit my website more information and free resources to assist you, or to find out how you can get in touch with a personal coach who can work with you.

Chapter 6

RULE #3: Reinvest Your Earnings

"I have a problem with too much money. I can't reinvest it fast enough, and because I reinvest it, more money comes in. Yes, the rich do get richer." ~ Robert Kiyosaki

Until your investment dam is big enough to support you, you must support it. By paying yourself first, and living within your means, you will begin to see the savings and investments begin to pile up. You will actually start to progress up the scale of financial security to becoming:

- *Financially fit*
- *Financially secure*
- *financially independent, and*

- *financially free*

This will not happen automatically. Once you have enough money to invest and your investments begin to make money on their own, your investments can start working for you. You must then faithfully keep sending your money out to work by reinvesting what it earns back into the investment dam you are building. It is critically important that you keep reinvesting the money your investments are earning until your dam is truly big enough to look after you on its own.

The Secret of Investing

How to actually invest will be dealt with in greater detail in Book Three, but there is a secret to investing you should know now. The secret to investing does not ultimately lie in capital growth, although this may be an important intermediate step in helping to grow your overall wealth.

The real power is in knowing how to get your investments creating an abundant passive income stream, or *cash flow,* that over time replaces the earnings you make from your own labour. This is where true financial freedom lies! Each month you have your investment income arrive into your bank account, regardless of whether you show up to work or not.

So how do we get to this point?

"Compound interest is the eighth wonder of the world. He who understands it, earns it ... he who doesn't ... pays it." ~ Albert Einstein

Reinvest your Investment Earnings

This rule allows you to use the power of Compound Interest to work for you, rather than against you.

In this chapter I'll be discussing this principle in concept. In Book Three I'll be diving into the detail and practical application.

So what do I actually mean by both compound interest and reinvesting your investment earnings?

I'll try to illustrate what I mean with another saying….

The rich don't work for money…they have their money work for them!

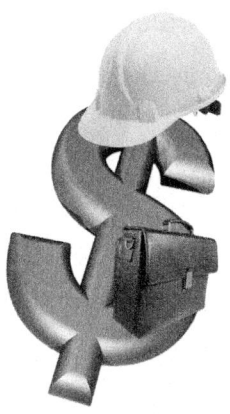

This is the whole point of the game of money...to have enough money working for you to give you the choice not to have to work for money yourself.

Okay, so you begin paying yourself first, and automatically making payments into your *PYF Account*...then what? This money starts earning interest, and eventually you begin to invest some of the money into investments that also make you money.

What do you do with the money your savings and investments make?

You must send this money back out to work as well. You can start by keeping it an interest bearing account until you get your next investment that makes you money. This will immediately mean that you now have more money working for you, making more money…and the money that it makes must be sent straight out to work as well. This is how you get the power of compound interest working for you.

The temptation to use the money can be strong, however if you do then you will seriously increase the amount of time it will take to become financially secure.

It can be very easy to look at the small about of money that your savings and investments make in the early days and underestimate the important of following Rule 3 – to reinvest this money.

Let me show you the power of reinvesting the earnings your investments make over time.
You may have seen the following example before, but please pay close attention.

If I said to you that I would give you one million dollars today, or give you 1 cent or penny and allow it to double every day for 30 days, which would you choose?

If you said 1 cent, well done – you understand the power of compound interest.

Let me show you:

Day	$1,000,000	1 Cent/Penny doubling every day
1	$1,000,000	$0.02
2	$1,000,000	$0.04
3	$1,000,000	$0.08
4	$1,000,000	$0.16
5	$1,000,000	$0.32
6	$1,000,000	$0.64
7	$1,000,000	$1.28
8	$1,000,000	$2.56
9	$1,000,000	$5.12
10	$1,000,000	$10.24
11	$1,000,000	$20.48
12	$1,000,000	$40.96
13	$1,000,000	$81.92
14	$1,000,000	$163.84
15	$1,000,000	**$327.68**
16	$1,000,000	$655.36

17	$1,000,000	$1,310
18	$1,000,000	$2,621
19	$1,000,000	$5,242
20	$1,000,000	$10,485
21	$1,000,000	$20,971
22	$1,000,000	$41,943
23	$1,000,000	$83,886
24	$1,000,000	$167,772
25	$1,000,000	$335,544
26	$1,000,000	$671,088
27	$1,000,000	**$1,342,177**
28	$1,000,000	$2,684354
29	$1,000,000	$5,368,708
30	$1,000,000	$10,737,417
Final Amount	**$1,000,000**	**$10,737,417**

If you had accepted the $1,000,000 upfront you would have cost yourself **$9,737,417!**

But take a close look – had you accepted the penny doubling, at day 15 you would only have **$327.84**. Your friends (and maybe yourself) would probably have been questioning your sanity.

In fact it took until day 27, or 90% of the month, to pass the $1 million dollar mark. This is the power of compound interest.

Okay, now I understand that you may look at the above example and say that it is not a true example of what could happen – first of all who would offer you such an opportunity, and you couldn't really expect to double your money every day. Fair enough – so let's look at a more realistic example:

Let's take a couple called Ken and Jen. They are both 35 years old, work full-time and between them bring home $100,000 per annum. They have made the decision to pay themselves first an amount equal to 20% of their take-home pay, i.e. $20,000 a year. Let's assume that they can invest it and get a yield or return of 8% per year on their investments. What would their investments look like over a 30-year period? We will look at the difference between if they decided to reinvest the earnings of their investments compared to if they decided to spend the earnings each year?

Year	*Spend* their Earnings	*Reinvest* their earnings
1	$20,000	$21,500
2	$40,000	$44,613
3	$60,000	$69,458
4	$80,000	$96,168
5	$100,000	$124,880
6	$120,000	$155,746
7	$140,000	$188,927
8	$160,000	$225,597
9	$180,000	$262,942
10	$200,000	$304,162
11	$220,000	$348,475
12	$240,000	$396,110
13	$260,000	$447,318
14	$280,000	$502,367
15	$300,000	$561,545
16	$320,000	$625,161
17	$340,000	$693,548
18	$360,000	$767,064
19	$380,000	$846,094
20	$400,000	$931,051
21	$420,000	$1,022,379

22	$440,000	$1,120,558
23	$460,000	$1,226,100
24	$480,000	$1,339,557
25	$500,000	$1,461,524
26	$520,000	$1,592,638
27	$540,000	$1,733,586
28	$560,000	$1,885,105
29	$580,000	$2,047,988
30	$600,000	$2,223,087
Final Amount	**$600,000**	**$2,223,087**

Can you see the power of Rule 3? If Ken and Jen had not followed Rule 3, and had chosen to spend the money their investments made rather than reinvest it, their investments would be $1,623,087 lower!

In the above example, *paying yourself first* (Rule 1) <u>AND</u> *reinvesting your earnings* (Rule 3) is 270% more powerful than just paying yourself first on its own!

Summary

So far we have covered the first 3 rules:

Rule 1 – Pay yourself first.

Rule 2 – Live within your means (on the money that is left after you have paid yourself first).

Rule 3 - Reinvest your investment earnings, until such time as you can or need to draw on that income stream in retirement.

I hope that the last few chapters have given you a clear understanding of these 3 rules, and how they work together to strengthen each other and make achieving financial security a goal that you truly can achieve.

This leaves us with one more rule to cover in this book:

Rule 4 – Protecting Yourself.

Chapter 7

RULE #4: Protect Yourself

"I declare to you that woman must not depend upon the protection of man, but must be taught to protect herself, and there I take my stand." ~ Susan B. Anthony

A key part of achieving financial peace of mind is to know that you have a safety net in place to protect you if anything goes wrong.

Despite our best plans, sometimes life can throw you a curve-ball. So the fourth rule is *Protect Yourself.*

This means protecting yourself and your family against whatever the future holds, as well as protecting your wealth as it grows.

In these books I'm talking about protecting yourself financially.

Ultimately the best protection will come from having strong portfolio of working investments that build an impenetrable financial wall around you and your family.

Until that time, however, an effective safety net is made up of two parts:

1. An Emergency buffer account; and
2. The right mix of insurances.

Emergency Buffer Account

This is having enough funds saved to cover a minimum of three months of your fixed expenses, and preferably between six and twelve months of cover. This will give you at least three months of safety net cover if needed in times of emergency or real need.

This is one of the first roles for your *PYF Account.* Note that it is vital that this is only used in times of real emergency, and no, an unbelievable never to be repeated end of year sale does not qualify as an emergency, nor does replacing tyres, or car registration, or any other annual expense that you didn't budget for.

We cover this is more detail in Book Three.

Insurance

Insurance is often thought of as a dirty word, with many people having been turned off by pushy salesmen. But having the right insurances in place is a vital part of your safety net until you are truly financially independent. There are two main categories of insurance:

1. General insurance

2. Personal insurance

General Insurance

General insurance includes such categories as:

- Home building and contents insurance
- Car Insurance
- Landlord insurance
- Travel Insurance
- Health Insurance
- Business Insurance

Most people have some level of home and contents, car, and health insurance and would feel quite vulnerable and exposed if they drove their car knowing that their insurance had expired. It is important to have the right amounts of general insurances in place, and I suggest that you review this annually to be sure that it remains suitable to your needs.

Personal Insurance

Personal Insurance breaks down into two main groups:

1. Income Protection insurance
2. Insurance that pays you cash lump sums

Income Protection

Income protection insurance protects your income earning ability. In Australia this can usually cover up to seventy-five percent of the income you earn from your personal exertion, if you are unable to work due to medical reasons. It can also cover a number of business expenses as well. Many countries around the world have equivalent types of insurance available.

This is a particularly vital insurance that is often overlooked. Your ability to earn an income is the key factor in being able to provide for your family today, as well as save for the future.

Ask yourself the following questions:

- QUESTION: If your income stopped today, how long could you keep living your current lifestyle?
- QUESTION: If your income stopped today, could you keep making your mortgage payments? For how long?
- QUESTION: If your income stopped today, could you keep *paying yourself first*, and not put your financial future at risk?

If your answer to any of the above questions is *no*, then you seriously need to consider getting income protection in place.

Cash Lump Sum Insurance

Insurances that give you cash lump sum payments generally include three categories:

1. Life Insurance: Pays a cash lump sum if you pass away whilst the insurance is in place.

2. Total and Permanent Disability Cover: Pays a cash lump sum if you are totally disabled and unable to ever return to work.

3. Trauma Cover: Pays a cash lump sum if you suffer a traumatic medical event or diagnosis that is on the list of insured events included in the coverage.

Did You Know?

The most common reason for retiring or permanently stopping work is poor health - particularly in those that have stopped working at a relatively young age (almost 80% of those who retired before forty-five years of age) (Source: ABS)

Insurance Objections

"I don't want to waste money on something I don't use!"

A huge number of Australians and Americans alike have too little insurance in place or none at all. The common objections are:

- *"It seems like such a waste of money!"*
- *"I've got better things to spend my money on!"*
- *"What are the chances that I actually need it?"*

Most of us know of or can think of people close to us who have had unexpected things happen to them, such as an accident, cancer, stroke or heart attack. Most of them did not expect anything bad to happen to them either, but it often happens without warning and is usually very traumatic to them (assuming they survive at least for a while) and their family. In particular it can have devastating financial consequences if the right safety nets aren't in place.

My sincere hope is that the money you spend on insurance turns out to be a complete waste, because this will mean that you have enjoyed a long and healthy life. However, we cannot be sure of that, so for this reason alone it is important to make sure that you and your family are covered against unexpected events.

"How much insurance cover do I really need?"

The answer to the question is just enough but not too much. You should also consider how much personal risk you want to be taking on yourself.

Calculating the right amount for you is a question for your financial adviser. He or she will look at a number of factors including:

- Lump sum amounts you want to make provision for, such as:
  o Debts to be paid out
  o Possible medical expenses
  o Possible legal and financial expenses
  o Provision for home and other lifestyle modification
- Ongoing income you would need.
- Your ability to self-insure (or what you currently own that you would be prepared to sell if the need arose).
- Your current health.

Your current health is one of the most compelling reasons to put insurance in place while you are still young and hopefully in good health. Once your insurance is in place, your insurer generally cannot cancel it, as long as you keep up with the payments.

As you build wealth you should progressively need *less* insurance as the gap that your safety net needs to cover gradually decreases as your financial assets increase.

Conclusion

"Any weapon is a good weapon as long as ye can use it with honor and skill."
~ Brian Jacques, High Rhulain

If you're feeling rejuvenated and excited to put the four pillars of wealth into action for yourself at this point, then you're right on track!

Many books end at this point, leaving you with perhaps a feeling of fulfillment and excitement but unaware that you have not developed the necessary skills, or even know specifically what to do yet. This is where Book Three – Your Path to Financial Freedom – comes in.

Book Three brings clarity around what to invest in together with the Four Pillars of Wealth.

In Book Three we will be covering topics that include:

- Terminating your debt;
- Building your buffer account;
- How to structure your bank accounts to work for you;
- The bucket method of investing for cash flow; and
- The Financially Fit Cash-Flow Management Program.

I then help you put it together into your own step-by-step *financial fitness* workout plan. The aim is that this plan will become just "the way things are done" around your home or office. The result will be that you will be on track to become *financially fit* within one to two months, and on a clear path to becoming financially free.

I look forward to seeing you again in Book Three!

To give you a look inside the next book in this series, I have included the Introduction for you to "Your Path to Financial Freedom."

Introduction

Welcome to Financially Fit.

This is the third book in the *Financially Fit* series. The previous two books were written to lay the foundation for getting you to this point.

In the first book – *How to Cure Money Stress* - we looked at the money mistakes that you must avoid if you wish to have any chance of becoming financially fit, and ultimately financially free.

In the second book – *"30 days to Financial Fitness"* - we discussed the four pillars of wealth. These are the four key principles that underlie any successful journey towards financial freedom.

In this book we get down into the specifics. This is where the rubber hits the road!

While it can certainly be read as a stand-alone, you will be at an advantage if you have read the first to book before jumping into this one.

Here we will be building on the principles from the first books, and tying it all together into a step-by-step plan. The goal is nothing less than for you to have a clear path to follow that will take you to *Financial Independence* and on to *Financial Freedom*.

What can you expect to get out of this book?

I've broken this book up into several parts.

We begin with getting a clear picture of what it is that you are building.

I repeat - the goal for you is to achieve nothing less than true financial freedom. But what does that actually look like?

Has anyone ever shown you exactly what *Financial Freedom* really looks like?

Well in part one I'm going to show you.

It is vital that you can clearly see what it is you are trying to achieve. Having a clear picture in your mind exponentially increases your chance of success.

In the second part, I'll be showing you exactly how you build your financial dream by graduating through each of the four stages of Financial Health.

I will be covering such things as:

- exactly where your savings should go
- how to structure your bank accounts so that they work for you
- whether you should get out of debt, or build wealth first
- how to terminate your debts with extreme prejudice
- what you should be investing in, and
- how to build wealth and achieve freedom.

By the end of this book you should be able to see a clear path from where you are today through to your dream lifestyle.

You will also be able to convert it into a step-by-step financial plan (and know exactly where you need to start today).

I don't promise that it will be easy. Like any fitness plan you should expect some degree of discomfort and discipline until the workouts become a habit.

What I do promise though is that the plan will be simple, and it works!

I have had the absolute pleasure of helping people turn their financial lives around by taking these *exact same steps* that I will be working through with you in this book.

If you are prepared to pay the price of discipline to put the plan into action for yourself, you will definitely start to become financially fitter and stronger within a matter of days.

Let's begin.

By the Author

Dr. Tony Pennells M.B.B.S, Dip. FS

 og

Books

Financially Fit - Book One: How to Cure Money Stress

Financially Fit - Book Two: 30 Days to Financial Fitness

Financially Fit - Book Three: Your Path to Financial Freedom

Connect with me!

I love getting feedback from my readers and would really appreciate you taking a few minutes to post your comments or a brief review on my Amazon page.

https://www.amazon.com/author/drtonypennells

Also come join our Facebook community here:

Facebook - www.facebook.com/finfitwithdrtony

Thank you!

CPSIA information can be obtained
at www.ICGtesting.com
Printed in the USA
LVOW04s1545061215
465638LV00031B/1364/P